Vendor Events
A How to Guide for Your Business

Vendor Events
A How to Guide for Your Business

By: Olive Watts

CONTENTS

INTRODUCTION

Are you building a new business?

Want to increase your business exposure?

Are you a seasoned business owner looking for fresh ideas?

Would you like to maximize your time? Save money?

If so, this is the book for you. Welcome!

This book will walk you through the details you need to rock a vendor event. We cover the following:

- How to select a vendor event –including ways to find events and important questions to ask

- How to prepare for an event – including strategies that make your business unique and memorable

- Important considerations for event day

- How to maximize your impact after an event

- And much much more…

While reading, you will notice a couple things.

First, I use bulleted lists. Why? Three reasons:

1. Ready-made TODO list – enough said.

2. Manageable bites – Rome wasn't built in a day and neither is a solid business. Simply move your way through each step in this book and you'll be a vendor event pro before you know it.

3. Skim reading – this style allows you to simply scan and quickly find the information you need.

Second, I encourage individuality.

There are many ways to peel a carrot. It is this diversity that makes life beautiful.

Use this book as a guide to pave your own successful path into the vendor event arena for your business. Acknowledge the unique skills, gifts, and strengths that you have to offer with your business then apply the information offered.

Please use what fits for you and your business then leave the rest. Each business is different and this guide has a lot of information. As you grow and adapt in your business, return for fresh ideas and inspiration.

As you read through each section, circle bullets that speak to you and fit well with your personality, strengths, and business. Explore those areas first, expanding on the ideas provided. By leveraging your strengths, you are naturally growing your business in a way that is uniquely you and that is beautiful.

CHAPTER 1 – CHOOSE AN EVENT

Ready to take your business to the next level with a vendor event?

In this section, we explore what it takes to choose an event that is right for you and your business:

- Find available events

- Ask questions

- Evaluate

- Register

Find Available Events

Events are everywhere just waiting to be discovered. Not sure where to start? This is the right section for you. We'll review the following:

- Who to ask

- Where to look for upcoming events

- Types of events available.

As you read through this section, circle bullets that speak to you and fit well with your personality, strengths, and business. Explore these areas first as you are searching for an event. By leveraging strengths, you are naturally growing your business in a way that is uniquely you.

Who to ask:

- Friends, family, neighbors
- Businesses in your niche
- Chamber of commerce
- Event planner/community organizer
- Event reporter for your local media outlet
- Business network and clients

Where to look for upcoming events:

- News media (TV, newspaper, magazine, online, ect.)
- Clubs/member organization gatherings and events
- Google search
- Social media
- Craigslist
- Local meetups
- Online communities – find groups or message boards that post upcoming events or vendor event opportunities in your community.
- Local bulletin boards at the library, coffee shop, church, ect.
- Event center – this could be the well known convention center in your city, local hotel, or even nursing home community room.

Types of events available:

- Convention/Expo

- Fundraiser

- Holiday

- Specialty association meeting

- Holiday/Seasonal Bazaar

- And much much more…

Ask Questions

Determine if the event is the right fit for your business by asking the right questions. In this section, we'll review common questions that gather the information you need to evaluate and plan for an event.

Questions are bundled into eight basic categories:

- Audience

- Event Promotion

- Business Promotion

- Price

- Location

- Other Vendors

- Event Coordinator

- Contracts

As you read through this section, circle bullets that you find most relevant to your business, local area, and niche. Each event and business is different, so not all questions may apply to your situation. Consider this list as a great starting point, adding additional questions as necessary to fit your specific needs.

Audience:

- How many people are estimated to attend the event?
- Who is estimated to attended the event?
    - o Ideally you should be able to easily describe this group in at least two words (gender, age, demographic, ect.).
- What are common interests of this audience?
- Does this audience fit the niche you want to attract to your business?

Event Promotion:

- How is the event marketed/promoted?
- Are attendees charged to enter the event?
    - o If so, ask for complimentary tickets to share.
- Does this promotion strategy appeal to the anticipated event audience? My target audience?

Business Promotion:

- Can my business be included in the event marketing material?
    - o If so, how is it promoted and is there a fee?
- Does the event have speaking/demonstration opportunities available?
- Can information about my business be share on the event email list, social media, ect.
- Is there a way for me to share promotional material in an event give away or goodie bag?

Price:

- What is the event fee?
    - If your experience or budget tells you the fee suggested is not reasonable for your business, try negotiating for a lower price.
- What size spots are available?
- What is included in the event fee (tent, table, table covering, electricity, internet, ect.)?
- Are any special discounts available (early registration, membership, ect.)?

Location:

- Outdoors or indoors?
- Is the location well known or easy to find?
- Can I setup early? If so, at what time and how secure is the area?

Other Vendors:

- Can I choose my display location?
- Are duplicate companies allowed? Duplicate products?
    - Do not hesitate to ask for exclusivity here, regardless of the response.
- How many vendors are expected?
- Is a list of vendors attending available (even if tentative or partial)?
    - This answer will be key when creating a unique event strategy. More on this in chapter two.

Event Coordinator:

- Has this event been held before? If so, was it at the same location?

- Has the coordinator managed other similar events?

- Are vendor references available?

GOLDEN NUGGET: Fully evaluate the event and coordinator before providing any form of payment – especially if you do not have a personal connection with the event, organization, or location. Consider personally calling a facility to verify the advertised event is scheduled with your coordinator.

Contracts

- What is required to reserve a vendor spot?

- Is a deposit required? If so, how much?

- Can I be added to the contact list for future events?

- What is the event's cancellation policy?

GOLDEN NUGGET: Some events may require tax information. The way you report this information may vary depending on your business and location involved. Please seek advice from the coordinator or your tax/legal professional.

Evaluate

Now, the decision is in your hands.

Review the answers you gathered to the questions above and critically evaluate if the event is a good fit for your business:

- What are the risks?

- What are the opportunities?

- Do the opportunities outweigh the risks?

- Does this event help you meet overall business goals?

Sometimes the answer is an obvious yes or no, but not always.

Lean on your resources when you are on the fence. Here are a few I use:

- Trusted friend
- Business advisor
- Pray/meditate
- Sleep on it
- Step away and return with a fresh perspective
- Research more

If the event is a good match, great! Move along to the next section. If not, take a minute to identify what does not fit for you. Keep these things in mind when searching and considering future events.

Register

You've searched, questioned, and evaluated…now you are ready to register!

Contact your event coordinator ASAP to confirm your interest and submit your application (including deposit, if applicable).

Vendor spots fill quickly. If there is not a space available for you, ask to be placed on a wait list or the coordinator's mailing list for future events.

CHAPTER 2 - PREPARE

Now what? In this section, we explore what it takes to prepare for a vendor event.

We'll review the following:

- Event Strategy
- Recruit Help
- Display
- Promote
- Supplies
- Communication Strategy
- Contact Strategy

As you move throughout this section, remember you know how you run your business best.

Use this information as a guide, shaping strategies provided for your unique business. The more unique the strategy, the more you are set apart from any competition.

Most preparation for an event does not happen overnight. Give yourself extra time to prepare and have fun.

Event Strategy

Attendees hear many messages on the day of the event. Make sure your business stands out by creating a strategy and message to match the event.

Start by asking yourself the following questions:

- Who is my audience?

    This question may have already been answered in chapter one above.

- What problem does my audience face?

    Not sure? Do a little research. Understand how the audience thinks, general concerns in the community, and recent topics of interest by reviewing media and influencers in their community.

- How does my product solve this problem?

    If you have multiple answers to this question, great. Write them all down.

- What will other vendors be saying?

    Pull out your list of other vendors attending the event.

    Consider what products and messages they may offer the audience.

    Do a little research and learn more about the other businesses. If it is close to the event date, you may even find some event specific marketing messages they are using.

- What unique solution does my business offer for this specific audience?

    > Compare the products and solutions you have available to the message/products other vendors are offering.

    > Make your message stand out by solving a core problem for your audience in a way that is specifically unique to your business.

Shape this unique solution into a message and strategy for the vendor event.

The goal of this strategy is to meet your event goals. It should fit with a message you and your business can honestly stand behind and support. The more comfortable and confident you feel about this plan, the better.

Use this event strategy to shape the rest of your event planning. Reach out to others for feedback and shift your ideas as needed.

Recruit Help

Plan to recruit some help for the event. A minimum of two people is helpful for the following reasons:

- When your display is busy, an extra voice available to offer one-on-one contact to attendees is critical.

- Supplies can be broken, forgotten, or lost – helpers can be your extra hand available to run errands offsite.

- When you are speaking or conducting a demo, a helper is available to continue assisting attendees at the display.

- Two words: Bathroom break.

Things to consider:

- Evaluate the event length (hours and days), display size reserved, and number of attendees expected to estimate the number of helpers you need.

- Plan ahead wisely – ask and schedule helpers in advance.

- Create shifts to give helpers (and yourself) breaks throughout the event.

- Choose helpers based on their knowledge of your business and ability to connect with your event audience.

- Clearly communicate your event strategy and goals to all helpers before the event.

Display

Vendor event displays are a great way to showcase the unique style of your business. Use your display to allow your business and strategy to shine.

Consider the following tips when designing your event display:

- Less is more.
    - o Have a simple, direct message – attendees are more likely to remember you.
    - o Only display items relevant to your strategy. When you find an attendee interested in other items your business offers, continue the discussion at the event and offer an opportunity to meet one-on-one for further discussion. This is a great way to build relationships.

- Leverage the power of three.
  - o Place three items together in a triangular shape. Use products, marketing materials, or props to achieve this balance.
  - o Use varied height levels throughout your display.
- Tell a story.
  - o Use banners, props, and products to tell a story about a solution your business provides. Design this story to directly communicate your event strategy.
  - o Divide display into sections that each tells a section of the story.

    [right side] Display a problem

    [middle] Give a solution

    [left side] Show the outcome
- Entertain.
  - o Plan fun entertainment or an engaging experience. This is a great way to spark a relationship with attendees. The sky is the limit here – use your event strategy and leverage your business strengths to create a unique experience.

    GOLDEN NUGGET: If you have multiple entertaining experiences planned, create a schedule and post it. This is an incentive that encourages attendees to return to your display.
- Spark Curiosity.
  - o Plan subtle elements that draw interest to your display:

- Use a textured fabric (such as fur) to encourage "feels" as attendee's pass and highlight an area of interest.
- Display a product that will spark curiosity and conversation.

- Bring nature inside.
  o Add a plant, flowers, or other natural elements in your display to renew your space with fresh vibrancy.

- Consider weather.
  o Attendees need to be comfortable at your display. Plan accordingly for a variety of weather conditions (wind, rain, sun, heat, chill, ect.).

- Presentation matters.
  o Give a clean/crisp presence with a wrinkle-free solid color tablecloth that reaches the ground on all sides.
  o Remove all elements that distract from your product and event strategy.

- Be known.
  o Use an easel, banner, or branded tablecloth to display your business name.
  o Make your business strategy or name obvious at a distance.

Practice setting up your display before the event.

Play around with the items displayed, where they are located, ect. Keep a balance of aesthetics and functionality – taking into consideration the number of helpers on hand.

Ask for feedback on your display – up close, far away, and as a passerby.

Promote

Connect with both loyal customers/fans and potential attendees through your promotion efforts. Save time and money by following established marketing methods that are successful for your business or try a fresh, new approach.

Here are some promotion channels to consider:

- Press coverage

- Social media

- Write an article or blog

  o Share with influencers in your event's target audience

- Ads (online and print)

- Word of mouth

- Local online message board/event calendars

- Email blasts

You're key here is to let others know you're attending the event and give them a reason to visit.

Generate a fresh buzz by promoting your business creatively. Use the strategy developed the first section of this chapter to connect with attendees and run with it.

Here are a few ideas to get started:

- Share the unique message you plan to deliver at the event – this is likely connected to your event strategy.

- Explain why this message is important – supporting articles and research can be helpful here.

- List other vendors and activities that are expected at the event. Highlight a favorite or two.

- o   This gives your audience more reason to attend and generates good vendor karma.
- Share the event schedule.
  - o   Make sure attendees know in advance where to be and when for your speaking or entertaining activities.
- Share your specials
  - o   Light that flame of desire to visit your display early with an event specific special. Consider having an early bird special to really spark the buzz.

Event coordinators are often looking for content and fresh ways to create buzz about their event. Give your business visibility a boost by sending promotional material to your event coordinator for sharing before, during, and after an event.

Supplies

When planning supplies for an event, it is best to plan your divide your efforts into three different phases:

- Plan
- Order
- Pack

Plan

Now is the time to plan what you need to achieve your marketing strategy. Consider the strategies you develop in Sections 3 and 4 to guide your planning here.

If your strategy includes a game or interactive/entertaining experience, invite a small audience (preferably similar to your event audience) over for a trial run. This provides an opportunity to practice and gather feedback. Watch for feedback or unexpected reactions then shift, plan, and improve as necessary.

<u>Order</u>

Allow enough time to design and order any marketing materials you may need for the event. Materials specific to your event strategy are a plus. Here are some basic materials you want to consider:

- Business cards

- Product brochures

- Quick reference information cards

- Large display banners

<u>Pack</u>

All of your supplies need to be at the vendor event on time. How you achieve this goal is up to your personal style. You may work best with a detailed list or prefer to just wing it - only you know how you work best.

Here are some common items I find useful to pack for an event:

- Display supplies
  - o Details are covered in the *Display* section of this chapter.
- Marketing supplies
  - o Include all of the great information you designed and ordered for the event.
- Sales supplies
  - o If you plan to have sales at your display, pack supplies you need to complete a transaction:
    - ▪ Receipt book

- Cash box/bag (with extra bills for change)
- Credit card reader

- Products
  - Pack only the products that you need for the strategy you defined.
  - If your goal does not include selling product, less is more here. Give attendees a taste of what is available and plan to share more at a later time. This makes your display less cluttered and save your back hauling products.

- Gifts
  - Are you offering a special gift for a special action during the event? If so, make sure they are beautifully packaged and readily available for handout.

- Business Event Binder
  - This is a binder that contains handy & easy to reference information you need for the event. Fill it with the following:
    - Product information. Use as a resource to answer questions you do not know offhand. Make copies so you can easily share.
    - Personal copy of event contract
    - Directions to the event & coordinator contact information
    - Personal calendar
    - State sales tax certificate (if needed)

- A few sheets of colored and white paper for a quick last-minute sign or note.

  GOLDEN NUGGET: Consider keeping this information in digital format.

- Mini-Office Kit
  - I use a small zippered pouch with 2 pens, 1 highlighter, 1 black sharpie, a pair of scissors, tape, hole punch, string, and post-it notes. This kit makes office products easy to find.

- Snacks & Water
  - It is important to stay hydrated through out the event to keep your brain active and alert, so pack plenty of water.
  - Choose snacks with little individual bites like dried fruit, nuts, sliced veggies, ect. If it requires a napkin or two hands to eat – leave it at home.

  GOLDEN NUGGET: Plan to eat before arriving to the event to avoid hunger cravings.

As you are packing for your event, keep all like items together in their own separate container/box. This makes it easier to find things before, during, and after an event. It also saves time during setup and tear down.

Items can be categorized into the following groups:

- Products
- Business needs (marketing materials, sales slips, money bank, ect.)
- Display props
- Personal Items (snacks/water, coat, purse, ect.)

Communication Strategy

Prior to an event, take some time to develop a communication strategy by brainstorming ways to effectively deliver your event strategy from chapter two:

- Plan casual guiding questions to encourage attendees to talk about topics relevant to your product.

- Practice delivering your message in a clear and simple way.

Leverage your strengths and methods that work best for your unique personality.

If you are speaking or leading a demo at the event, now is the time write and prepare your presentation. Successful presentations:

- Provide value.

- Speak directly to audience needs.

- Showcase your businesses specific personality.

When finished with a presentation, invite the audience to continue the discussion by visiting your display.

Contact Strategy

Gathering attendee contact information is one of the many benefits of having a vendor event display. Use your time effectively by developing a strategy that speaks to attendees and matches your business style.

Attendees that pass by your display typically fall into one of five categories:

- Ready to buy your product

- Interested in learning more

- Willing to attend a future event of yours

- Not interested and would like a freebie

- Not interested

Attendees are most willing to share their contact information for a specific purpose. A great contact strategy considers the following questions:

- Who do you want to contact?

- How will you contact them?

- What is the most effective way to collect their information?

Make the process of collecting attendee information quick and simple. Use an approach that resonates best with your audience:

- Simple signup sheet on a clipboard or drawing entry slip. Ask for name, email, ect.

- Ask survey questions (in addition to the signup above).

    o Ask about product preference, gauge interest in classes/events, ect.

    o This is a great option if you (or a helper) are not available to directly communicate with all people that visit your display.

- Ask to "Like" or "Follow" you on social media.

- Online registration form – available via link, QR code, laptop, or iPad.

Have a busy life after you leave an event? Prepare a welcome email or newsletter for your new contacts before the event starts. Then all you need to do is upload the new contact information and send.

Here are a few fun things to mention in your welcome email:

- Send thanks – appreciate all people that stopped by your display and coordinators of the event.

- Include product information from your display – including handouts as attachments.

- Share your specials – send a reminder before a sale or special ends.

- Create a feeling of celebrity by publicly congratulating winners of your giveaway.

GOLDEN NUGGET: Offer gifts to all that registered, such as 50% off coupon for an upcoming class.

- Share upcoming events for your business.

GOLDEN NUGGET: Plan & schedule additional opportunities to engage with attendees after an event. Offer free or paid events as a way to "continue the conversation" and invite them to learn more in a low-pressure environment.

CHAPTER 3 – DO IT

It is the day of the event. Ready to rock it?

In this section, we'll cover the following:

- Arrive & Setup
- Connect with Attendees
- Promote
- Gather Contacts
- Reflect
- Pack up

Arrive & Setup

Expect the best and prepare for the worst. Not everything may flow as planned and that is okay – be flexible and shift as needed to meet your changing environment.

Arrive to the event early, allow enough time to setup your display as practiced and get comfortable in the space.

You may notice early attendees and other vendors walking around the event space checking out vendor displays during setup time. This crowd is usually pretty social. Have your display setup early so you can give them your full attention.

Connect with Attendees

Your communication strategy, created in chapter two, starts the moment you arrive to the event venue.

Radiate a welcoming and uplifting attitude – before, during, and after the event. Other vendors notice and remember, so do event attendees.

Guide a genuine and productive connection with attendees at your event by following this four-step process:

1. Entertain.

    - Execute your entertainment strategy as a fun/casual way to welcome attendees to your display.

2. Watch the attendee and pay attention – notice attributes that you give you insight into their perspective and how they may use the product/service you are offering.

    GOLDEN NUGGET: Use caution and sensitivity when communicating using any observations.

3. Listen, listen, listen.

    - Most attendees want to tell their story and how they think they relate to your products. Listen and appreciate what they have to say. This story gives you critical insight into how your product best serves their specific needs.

4. Guide the conversation.

    - Don't do all the talking (see previous step: listen, listen, listen)

- Ask open-ended questions relevant to the attendee.

  EXAMPLE DIALOG:

  Have you ever experienced XYZ product?

  If yes, "Oh great, what do you like most about it?"

  If no, ask an open-ended question relating to your event message theme or observation about their interests.

- Build a bridge.
  - o Create a bridge between what the attendee understands and the product you offer:
    - Identify a problem that you can help resolve.
    - Demonstrate or explain the solution.
    - Outline additional benefits of the solution.

Here are some additional success strategies to consider:

- Stand beside or in front of your display to create a personal connection and comfortably communicate with attendees.
- Be friendly.
- Be open to asking, "Do you want to meet to discuss more?"
  - o This is a great way to continue the conversation and build the relationship in a quieter one-on-one environment.

o Gather their contact information and schedule a date/time to meet.

GOLDEN NUGGET: Aim for 24-48 hours after the event, the sooner the better.

- Invite attendees to an upcoming class or event for your business.

    o Vendor events are great ways to advertise other upcoming events and activities.

    o Collect payment to ensure commitment for class registrations.

Promote

Promote your business online throughout the event to keep your people informed:

- Share photos of attendees interacting with your business on social media. Make sure to include any fun entertainment activities you've prepared.

- Throughout the event, make and post video testimonial reviews or attendee interviews.

- Share your specials – consider offering a surprise "power hour" special that is only available for a specific hour of the event.

Give attendees reasons to promote your business:

- Hand out brightly colored or visible swag that matches the style of your business, event strategy, or display theme:

    o Bags

    o Balloons

    o Flowers (real or paper)

    o Stickers

- o Hats

- o ect. the sky is the limit here.

GOLD NUGGET: Aim for ways to spark curiosity for those that have not yet attended your display.

- Encourage attendees to take and post photos from your display via social media – cardboard face cutout anyone?

- Create a contest with an incentive for attendees to actively promote your business.

GOLD NUGGET: Consider teaming up with the event coordinator and other vendors to create a scavenger hunt for attendees.

Gather Contacts

Gather contacts throughout the event by following your strategy from chapter two.

The more information you have on your contacts, the better. This is especially true if your strategy includes individual one-on-one contact. Keep additional notes on specific contact to track product preferences, interests, or key contacts for future marketing efforts.

Once you have attendee contact information, here are a few general rules of thumb:

- Reach out to your attendee while the experience is still fresh in their mind - follow up within 24-48 hours.

- Keep leads and their preferences categorized.

  - o Increase your rate of conversion by sending out marketing messages aimed directly at specific preferences – this is especially helpful if your product appeals to a variety of different niches or you offer a multiple services.

GOLDEN NUGGET: Keep your eyes open for attendees that could be a great referral. Offer incentives for referring an interested friend, spouse, or coworker to learn more about your business or product.

Reflect

Throughout the day, take a step back to see how you are doing:

- How successful is your event strategy?
- Are you connecting with attendees?
- Are you achieving your goals for the event?

If so, congratulations!

If not, shift and change what you need to best meet your environment. Remember, you are a rock star!

Pack Up

I am habitually one of the last vendors to pack up…and for very good reason.

The sheer scarcity of the closing event frequently triggers attendees to make a quick purchase or action. When your display is one of the last available to check out, final lingering attendees naturally gravitate in your direction.

CHAPTER 4 –END ON A HIGH NOTE

Your event is over – Congrats!

Now what? Close our your event in style by following our favorite trio checklist within 24-48 hours after an event:

- Thanks

- Reach out

- Evaluate

Thanks

Send out a thank you to all that contributed toward your event. Consider those that helped you prepare materials, helped work in your display, or family that provided moral support. Each vendor event takes energy and effort – show your appreciation all around with an attitude of gratitude to those around you and yourself.

Reach out

Event attendees have just had a fun time at the vendor event; don't let the conversation end there.

Take advantage of your buzzing energy to enter contacts you collected into a welcome email or newsletter. Send within 24-48 hours of event. Your contacts are looking forward to hearing from you!

GOLDEN NUGGET: Unsure of what to include in the welcome message? Check out chapter two for some suggestions.

Evaluate success

Take some time to evaluate the event. I like to do this in a comfortable setting the evening after an event.

Here are a few questions to get you started:

- Did you achieve your goals?
- Will you do that specific event again?
- What will you improve next time you have an event?
- What will you keep the same?

List three of each:

- Successes
- Favorite moments from the event
- Areas to Improve
- Things to do next time

This is great information to record in a journal as it is helpful to reflect on as your business grows and changes in the future.